CLASSICAL THEMES FOR TWO

Arrangements by Peter Deneff

ISBN 978-1-5400-1412-2

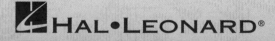

7777 W. BLUEMOUND RD. P.O. BOX 13819 MILWAUKEE, WI 53213

In Australia Contact:
Hal Leonard Australia Pty. Ltd.
4 Lentara Court
Cheltenham, Victoria, 3192 Australia
Email: ausadmin@halleonard.com.au

Visit Hal Leonard Online at
www.halleonard.com

ACADEMIC FESTIVAL OVERTURE

CLARINETS

By JOHANNES BRAHMS

Slowly

AIR
from WATER MUSIC

CLARINETS

By GEORGE FRIDERIC HANDEL

Andante con moto

(small notes optional)

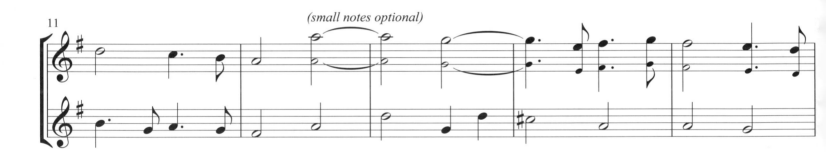

To Coda

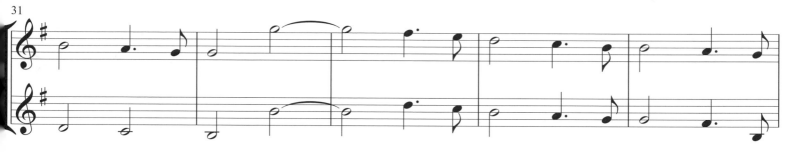

CODA

D.C. al Coda

rit.

AIR ON THE G STRING

from ORCHESTRAL SUITE NO. 3 IN D MAJOR, BWV 1068

CLARINETS

By JOHANN SEBASTIAN BACH

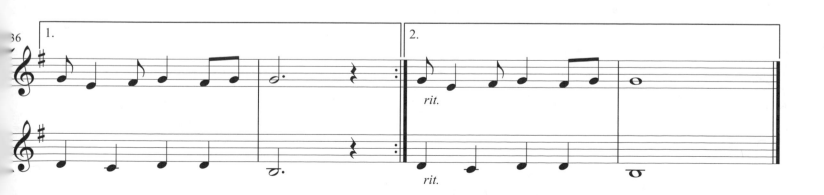

BLUE DANUBE WALTZ

CLARINETS

By JOHANN STRAUSS, JR.

Moderately

CANON IN D

CLARINETS

By JOHANN PACHELBEL

CLAIR DE LUNE
from SUITE BERGAMASQUE

CLARINETS

By CLAUDE DEBUSSY

Andante

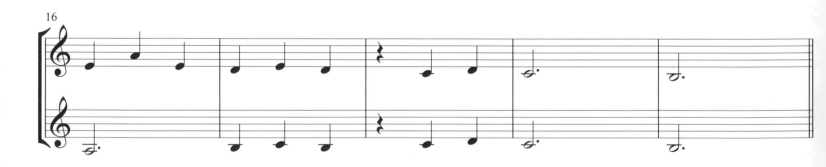

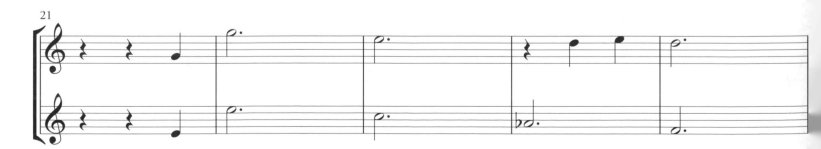

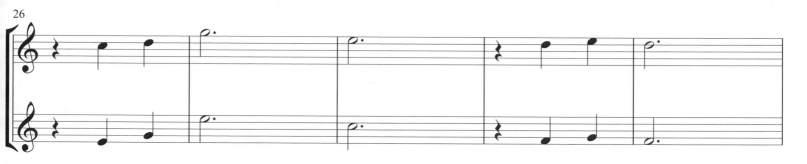

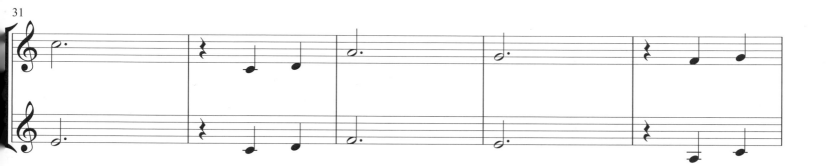

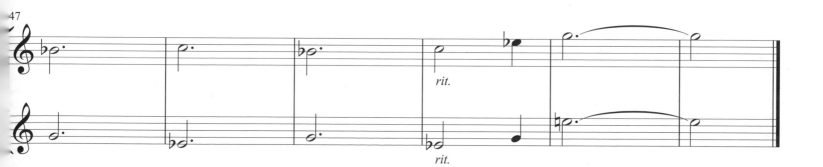

EINE KLEINE NACHTMUSIK
(Second Movement Theme: "Romance")

CLARINETS

By WOLFGANG AMADEUS MOZART

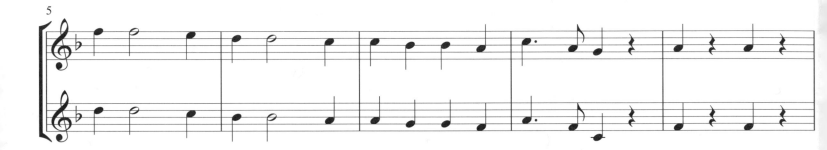

FLOWER DUET
from LAKMÉ

CLARINETS

By LÉO DELIBES

Andante con moto

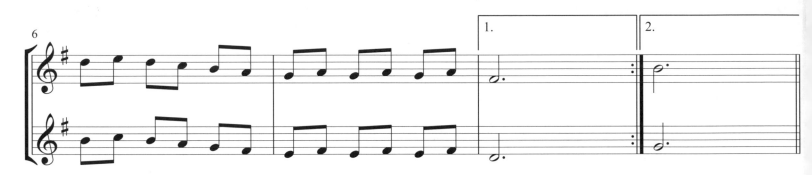

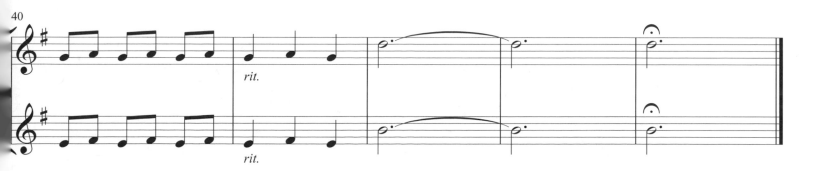

HALLELUJAH CHORUS
from MESSIAH

CLARINETS

By GEORGE FRIDERIC HANDEL

Allegro

25

(small note optional)

30

34

38

42

47

rit.

HORNPIPE
from WATER MUSIC

CLARINETS

By GEORGE FRIDERIC HANDEL

Allegro maestoso

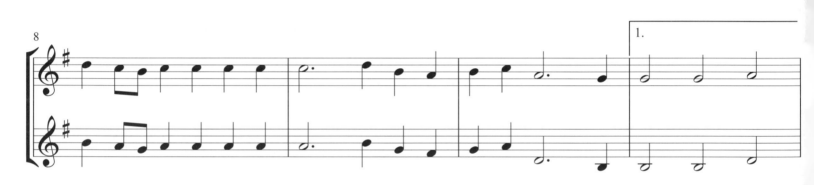

HUNGARIAN DANCE NO. 5

CLARINETS

By JOHANNES BRAHMS

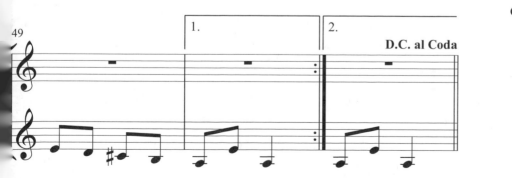

JESU, JOY OF MAN'S DESIRING
from CANTATA 147

CLARINETS

By JOHANN SEBASTIAN BACH

Moderately

D.C. al Coda

CODA

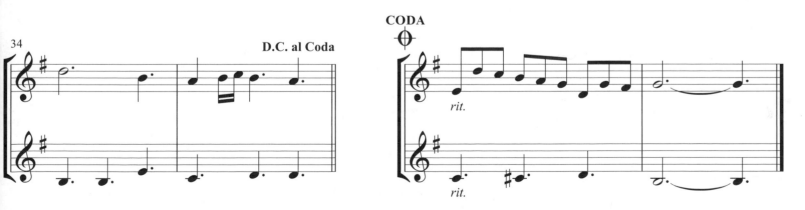

rit.

rit.

MARCH
from THE NUTCRACKER

CLARINETS

By PYOTR IL'YICH TCHAIKOVSKY

March tempo

MINUET IN G
from ANNA MAGDALENA NOTEBOOK

CLARINETS

By CHRISTIAN PETZOLD
formerly attributed to J.S. Bach

Moderately

ODE TO JOY
from SYMPHONY NO. 9 IN D MINOR

CLARINETS

By LUDWIG VAN BEETHOVEN

MORNING
from PEER GYNT

CLARINETS

By EDVARD GRIEG

Allegretto pastorale

PICTURES AT AN EXHIBITION
(Promenade)

CLARINETS

By MODEST MUSSORGSKY

POMP AND CIRCUMSTANCE
March No. 1

CLARINETS

By EDWARD ELGAR

Allegro

RONDEAU
from SUITE DE SYMPHONIE

CLARINETS

By JEAN-JOSEPH MOURET

Moderately

SHEEP MAY SAFELY GRAZE

from CANTATA 208

CLARINETS

By JOHANN SEBASTIAN BACH

Andante

THE SURPRISE SYMPHONY
(Symphony No. 94, Second Movement Theme)

CLARINETS

By FRANZ JOSEPH HAYDN

Andante

SYMPHONY NO. 7
(Second Movement Theme)

CLARINETS

By LUDWIG VAN BEETHOVEN

Allegretto

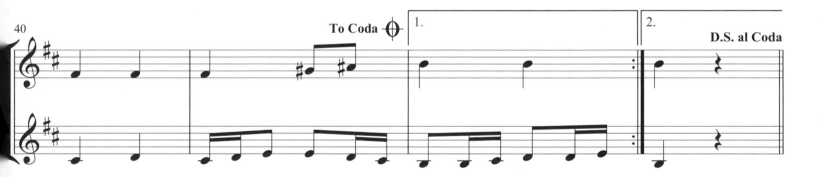

TRUMPET VOLUNTARY
(Prince of Denmark's March)

CLARINETS

By JEREMIAH CLARKE

WILLIAM TELL OVERTURE
(Theme)

CLARINETS

By GIOACHINO ROSSINI

Allegro vivace

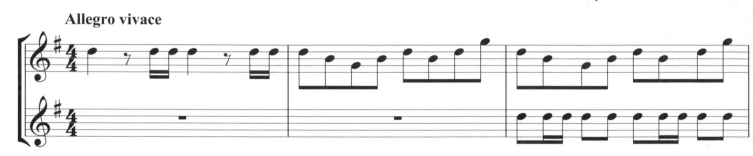